For Parents and Guardians:

This book is designed to teach children how to create their own web pages in a fun and educational way. However, we recommend that minors use this book under adult supervision. This is to ensure that they stay safe while browsing the internet and using various online tools.

For Children:

Hello little programmer! We are very happy that you are excited to learn how to create your own website. Before we start, we want to remind you of some important things to help you stay safe online:

- **Don't share personal information** : Never share your full name, address, phone number, or any other personal information on your website or with people you don't know.

- **Use safe images and content** : Make sure that any images or content you use are appropriate and that you have permission to use them. It's always best to use images that you created yourself or that you know are free and safe.

- **Ask an adult** : If you have any questions or find something you don't understand while following this book, don't hesitate to ask an adult for help. They are there to help you and make sure you have fun safely.

Have fun and learn!

Remember that security is the most important thing as you explore the wonderful world of web creation. We're excited to see what you're going to create !

Hello website builder!

Have you ever visited a website and wondered how it was created? Today is your lucky day! In this book, we are going to teach you how to create your own website from scratch. It doesn't matter if you've never done something like this before, here we will explain everything step by step and in a very fun way.

Imagine being able to show the world your interests, your hobbies, or even your favorite stories. You can design and build your own corner on the Internet where all your friends and family can visit you. You can even make a page for your pet, your friends club, or your school projects!

What will you learn?

- **What is a website** and why it's great to have yours.
- **How to plan my page web** : the first step towards your creation!
- **Tools and programs** that we will use, they are all free and easy to use.
- **Design and customize** your page to make it look amazing.
- **Add** content such as texts, images and videos.
- **Make your page interactive** with forms and comments.
- **Publish and share** your creation with the world.
- **Maintain and update** your page so that it is always up to date.

Each chapter is packed with examples and hands-on activities. Additionally, at the end of each section, you will find small missions to put into practice what you have learned. It's like a video game, but creating something real and yours!

Let us begin!

Let's not wait any longer! Let's embark on this digital adventure and discover how fun it is to create your own website. Are you ready? Let's go there!

Great, we're ready to start! But, before we get to work, it is important to understand well what a website is.

Imagine This :

Think of a web page as a **notebook** . In this notebook, you can write stories, draw pictures, share videos and much more. And best of all, this notebook can be viewed by anyone in the world who has access to the Internet. It's like having a giant showcase where you can show the world your ideas!

Parts of a Web Page

A web page has several important parts:

- **Title** : It is the name of your page. Imagine that it is the title of a book. It should be clear and attractive.

- **Text** : This is where you write your content. It can be a story, information about your favorite hobby, or anything you want to share.

- **Images** : Images make your page more interesting! You can use photos, drawings or graphics.

- **Links** : These are like bridges that take visitors to other web pages. You can link to videos, articles or anything you find interesting.

- **Videos** : Adding videos can make your page even more dynamic and fun.

- **Buttons and Menus** : These help your visitors navigate your page. It's like having road signs telling you where to go.

Why is it Great to Have a Website?

- **Share your Interests** : You can show your hobbies, like your game collections and gos , your drawings, or your favorite recipes.

-**Connect with Friends and Family** : Your website can be a place where your friends and family see what you are doing and leave comments.

- **Learn and Have Fun** : Creating a website is a great way to learn new skills while having fun. It's like playing and learning at the same time!

Web Page Example

Here's a simple example of what a web page might look like:

My Amazing Website

Title : "The World of Dinosaurs"

Text : "Welcome to my dinosaur page! Here you will find information about the most incredible dinosaurs that existed millions of years ago."

Images :

Links: "Click here to watch a video about the T- Rex " | "Visit this page for more information about dinosaurs"

Videos : [Video of T- Rex roaring]

Buttons and Menus : "Home" | "Gallery" | "Videos" | "Contact"

And that's how simple it is! Now that you know what a website is and why it's so great to have one, you're ready to start creating your own. Let's move on to the next chapter and start planning your amazing website!

Chapter 2 . How to Plan My Website?

You are about to start your exciting adventure creating your own website! But, like any big project, it's important to plan before you start. Here we show you how to do it in an easy and fun way.

Step 1: What Do You Want to Create?

First, think about the theme of your website. Here are some ideas to inspire you:

- **Personal Blog** : Share your stories, thoughts and adventures.

- **Hobbies Page** : Show your hobbies, such as collections, sports, or crafts.

- **School Project Page** : Present your projects and school work in a creative way.

- **Pet Page** : Share photos and anecdotes of your pets.

Activity: Brainstorming

Grab a piece of paper and a pencil, and answer these questions:

- What topic do I want to make my website about?

- What type of content do I want to include (texts, images, videos)?

- Who will be my visitors (friends, family, classmates)?

Step 2: Sketch of Your Website

Before you start working on the computer, it's helpful to make a sketch of what you want your website to look like. This will help you visualize where the different parts will go.

Activity: Draw your Sketch

1. **Title and Header** : Draw the title of your page and the header at the top.

2. **Main Sections** : Divide your page into sections (for example, "About Me", "Photo Gallery", "My Favorite Videos").

3. **Navigation Menu** : Add a menu at the top or side so visitors can easily move between sections.

4. **Main Content** : In each section, draw spaces for text, images and videos.

Step 3: Choose Your Style

Think about the style and   colors you want to use on your page. Here are some ideas:

- **Bright and Cheerful Colors** : Perfect for a page about hobbies or pets.

- **Neutral and Elegant Tones** : Ideal for a personal blog or a school project.

- **Fun and Creative Themes** : Use backgrounds and graphics that reflect your personality.

Step 4: Gather Materials

Now that you have a plan, start gathering the materials you will need:

- **Photos** : Take or search for photos you want to use.

- **Texts** : Write the texts you want to include (they can be stories, descriptions, etc.).

- **Videos** : If you plan to include videos, make sure you have them ready.

Step 5. Organize your time

Finally, organize your time to work on your website. You can make a weekly schedule and decide which parts you will work on each day.

Checklist to Plan your Website

1. **Theme** : Defined

2. **Sketch** : Drawn on paper

3. **Style and Colors** : Chosen

4. **Photos and Texts** : Reunited

5. **Schedule** : Organized

With these steps, you are now ready to start creating your website! In the next chapter, we'll show you how to choose the perfect platform and get started with the design. Let's go there!

To create your website, we are going to use some tools and programs that are free and easy to use. Here we present the main ones that we will use throughout this book.

Google Sites

What is it?

Google Sites is a free Google tool that allows you to easily create web pages.

Advantages :

- Easy to use, ideal for beginners.

- Integration with other Google services (Drive, Docs , Sheets , etc.).

- Pre-designed templates that you can customize.

How to Get Started :

1. Go to [Google Sites](https://sites.google.com).

2. Sign in with your Google account.

3. Click "Create" to start your new page.

Wix for Kids

What is it?

Wix is a popular platform for creating websites. It has a kid-friendly version with simple templates and tools.

Advantages :

- Drag and drop editor, easy to use.

- Colorful and fun templates.

- Extensive library of free images and graphics.

How to Get Started :

1. Go to [Wix](https://www.wix.com).

2. Create a free account.

3. Select a template and start customizing your page.

Weebly for Education

What is it?

Weebly is another website building platform, specially designed for students and teachers.

Advantages :

- Safe environment for children.

- Specific educational functionalities.

- Easy to use with customization options.

How to Get Started :

1. Go to [Weebly for Education](https://education.weebly.com).

2. Register as a student.

3. Choose a template and start designing your site.

canva

What is it?

Canva is an online tool for creating stunning visual graphics and designs.

Advantages :

- Intuitive and easy-to-use interface.

- Templates for all types of graphics (banners, logos, images).

- Library of images, icons and graphic elements.

How to Get Started :

1. Go to [Canva](https://www.canva.com).

2. Create a free account.

3. Explore the templates and start designing.

Pixabay

What is it?

Pixabay is a free image bank where you can find royalty-free photos and graphics.

Advantages :

- Great variety of high quality images.

- Free and without the need for attribution (although it is always a good idea).

- Easy to search and download.

How to Get Started :

1. Go to [Pixabay](https://pixabay.com).

2. Find the images you need.

3. Download the images and use them on your website.

1. **Explore the** Tools: Visit the websites of the tools mentioned and create free accounts that you don't have.

2. **Test the Features** : Take some time to explore and test the features of each tool.

3. **Save your Designs** : If you create any graphics or images in Canva , save it to use later on your website.

You are now ready to use all these tools and programs to create an amazing website! In the next chapter, we will begin to design and customize your website using the platforms you have chosen. Let's go !

Chapter 4 . Design Your Website

You now have a fantastic plan for your website and you know the tools and programs we will use! Now it's time to start bringing it to life on the computer. In this chapter, we will learn how to choose a platform and take the first steps in creating your website.

Choose your Platform

There are several free and easy-to-use platforms that we already mentioned to create your website. Here we   remind you of some great options:

1. **Google Sites**

    - **Advantages** : Easy to use, integration with other Google tools.

    - **How to Get Started** : Go to [Google Sites](https://sites.google.com) and use your Google account to get started.

2. **Wix for Kids**

    - **Advantages** : Colorful and fun templates, drag and drop editor.

    - **How to Get Started** : Go to [Wix](https://www.wix.com) and create a free account.

3. **Weebly for Education**

    - **Advantages** : Safe and designed for students, easy to use.

    - **How to Get Started** : Go to [Weebly for Education](https://education.weebly.com) and register as a student.

First steps

1. **Register and Create an Account**

   - Go to the platform you have chosen.

   - Follow the instructions to create an account. (Remember to ask an adult for help if you are a minor).

2. **Select a Template**

   - Templates are pre-made designs that you can customize. Choose one that you like and that suits your theme.

   - Explore the options and select the one that most appeals to you.

3. **Explore the Editor**

   - Take some time to familiarize yourself with the editor. Most platforms have a drag-and-drop interface, meaning you can click and drag elements (like text, images, and videos) onto your page.

Customize Your Template

1. **Add Your Title and Header**

   - Write the name of your page in the title.

   - Customize the header with an image or background color you like.

2. **Create the Main Sections**

   - Use the sketch you drew in a previous chapter to create the different sections of your page.

   - Add sections such as "About Me", "Photo Gallery", "My Favorite Videos".

3. **Add Initial Content**

- **Text** : Click on the text areas and write your descriptions, stories or information.

- **Images** : Upload the photos you have collected and place them in the corresponding sections.

- **Videos** : If you have videos, upload or insert the links.

Customize the Style

1. **Choose Colors and Fonts**

- Most platforms allow you to change colors and fonts. Choose a color scheme you like and make sure the texts are easy to read.

- Experiment with different fonts (typefaces) until you find the ones that best suit your style.

2. **Add Fun Elements**

- Use stickers, icons and graphics to make your page more attractive.

- Some platforms offer a library of visual elements that you can use.

Practical example

Here's an example of what your home page might look like:

Title : The World of Dinosaurs

Header :

Section 1: About Me

"Hello! I'm [Your Name] and I love dinosaurs. On this page you will find information about my favorite dinosaurs."

Section 2: Photo Gallery

[Photos of different dinosaurs]

Section 3: My Favorite Videos

[Links to dinosaur videos]

1. **Create your Account and Choose a Template**

2. **Customize the Title and Header**

3. **Add and Organize at Least Two Sections**

4. **Experiment with Colors and Fonts**

Fantastic job! Now your website is starting to take shape. In the next chapter, we'll show you how to add more content and make your page even more interesting. Let's move forward!

Your website is taking shape! Now it's time to add content and give it a unique style that reflects your personality and interests.

Write Your First Article

A good article should be informative and entertaining. Here is a guide to writing your first article:

1. **Choose a Topic** : It can be something you are passionate about, like your favorite hobby, an interesting story, or information about your pets.

2. **Make an Outline** :

    - **Title** : A striking title that captures the attention of readers.

    - **Introduction** : A short paragraph that introduces the topic.

    - **Body** : Several paragraphs with detailed information and examples.

    - **Conclusion** : A summary and an invitation to readers to leave comments or questions.

Example :

Title : "All about the T- Rex"

Introduction : "Tyrannosaurus Rex , or T- Rex , is one of the most well-known and feared dinosaurs of all time. In this article, you will discover fascinating facts about it incredible dinosaur."

Body :

- **Features** : "The T- Rex was approximately 12 meters long and weighed around 9 tons."

- **Habitat** : "It lived in North America about 68 million years ago."

- **Diet** : "He was a carnivore, which means he ate meat."

Conclusion : "The T- Rex remains one of the most fascinating creatures that ever existed. What's your favorite dinosaur? Leave me a comment and tell me!"

Add Images and Videos

Images and videos make your website more attractive and dynamic. Here we show you how to add them:

1. **Add Images** :

    - **Upload Images** : Use the "Upload" option to add photos from your computer.

    - **Use Free Images** : Sites like [Pixabay](https://pixabay.com) offer free images that you can use.

    - **Add Descriptions** : Write descriptions under each image to explain what they show.

2. **Add Videos** :

    - **Upload Videos** : If you have your own videos, you can upload them directly.

    - **Insert Links** : Copy and paste links from YouTube videos or other platforms.

Example of Visual Content:

Section: Photo Gallery

[Photos of the T- Rex in different poses]

Section: T-Rex Videos

[Link to YouTube video of the T- Rex roaring]

Text Styles

Using different text styles can make your content easier to read and more interesting.

1. **Titles and Subtitles** :

    - Use titles for important sections.

    - Add subtitles to divide the content into smaller parts.

2. **Bold and Italics** :

    - Use bold to highlight key words.

    - Use italics for book titles, scientific names, or to add emphasis.

3. **Lists and Bullets** :

    - Use lists to organize information.

    - Use bullet points to list items clearly and concisely.

Example :

Title : "Characteristics of the T- Rex"

Subtitle : "Size and Weight"

Text : "The **T- Rex** was approximately **12 meters** long and weighed around **9 tons**."

End of Chapter Activity

1. **Write an Article** : Follow the guide and write your first article.

2. **Add Images and Videos** : Upload at least one image and one video to your page.

3. **Experiment with Text Styles** : Use titles, subtitles, bold, italics and lists in your article.

Amazing work! Now your page has interesting and visually appealing content. In the next chapter, you will learn how to make your page interactive, adding links, forms and comments. Let's move forward!

Chapter 6: Make your Page Interactive

Your website already looks fantastic! Now we are going to make it even more interesting and fun by adding interactive elements. This will allow your visitors to actively participate on your page, leaving comments, filling out forms, and easily navigating between sections. Use the editor to add whatever you like.

Add Links

Links allow visitors to navigate between different sections of your website or visit other interesting websites.

1. **Internal Links** :

   - Use links to connect different sections of your website.

   - For example, you can add a link in the main menu that takes visitors to your photo gallery.

Example :

```html
Html                              Copiar código

<a href="#galeria">Galería de
Fotos</a>
```

2. **External Links :**

- Use links to direct visitors to other websites that are interesting or related to your content.

- For example, you can add a link to an educational video on YouTube.

Example :

```html
<a
href="https://www.youtube.com
/watch?v=video_id"
target="_blank">Mira este video
sobre el T-Rex</a>
```

Create Forms

Forms are a great way to collect information from your visitors, such as their names, emails, and comments.

1. **Contact Form** :

   - Create a simple form where visitors can send you messages.

   - Includes fields such as name, email and message.

Example:

```html
<form
action="tu_url_de_formulario"
method="post">
  <label for="nombre">Nombre:</
label><br>
  <input type="text"
id="nombre" name="nombre"><br>
  <label for="email">Correo
Electrónico:</label><br>
  <input type="email"
id="email" name="email"><br>
  <label
for="mensaje">Mensaje:</
label><br>
  <textarea id="mensaje"
name="mensaje"></textarea><br>
  <input type="submit"
value="Enviar">
</form>
```

2. **Surveys and Questionnaires** :

   - Use forms to create interactive surveys or questionnaires.

   - This can be a fun way to get your visitors' opinions on different topics.

Add Comments

Allowing your visitors to leave comments can make your page more interactive and engaging.

1. **Google Comment System Sites** :

   - If you use Google Sites , you can enable comments on sections of your page.

2. **Comments Widgets** :

   - Platforms like Wix and Weebly have comment widgets that you can easily add to your page.

   - These widgets allow visitors to leave their opinions and questions.

Insert Maps and Other Widgets

1. **Google Maps** :

   - If your page has a physical location, you can insert a Google map to show where it is located.

   - Go to Google Maps , search for the location, and copy the embed code.

Example :

```html
<iframe
src="https://www.google.com
/maps/embed?pb=
!1m18!1m12!1m3!1d...">
</iframe>
```

Html   📋 Copiar código

2. **Calendars :**

- Insert a calendar to show important events or special dates.

- You can use Google Calendar and copy the embed code.

3. **Social Network Widgets :**

- Add social media widgets so visitors can follow your profiles on Facebook, Twitter, Instagram, etc.

- These widgets are usually available in the customization options of your platform.

1. **Add Links** : Insert at least one internal and one external link on your page.

2. **Create a Contact Form** : Use the example provided to create a contact form.

3. **Enable Comments** : Add a comment system to one of your sections.

4. **Insert a Map or Widget** : Add a Google map, calendar, or social media widget to your page.

Excellent work! Now your website is interactive and your visitors can actively participate. In the next chapter, we will learn how to publish and share your website with the world. Let's go there!

Chapter 7: Publish and Share

Your website is ready! Now it's time to publish it and share it with the world. In this chapter, we will guide you through the steps to make your page visible on the internet and give you tips on how to share it with your friends, family, and colleagues.

Publish your Website

Depending on the platform you have chosen, the steps to publish your page may vary a little. Here we show you how to do it on some of the most popular platforms.

1. **Google Sites :**

    - Click the "Publish" button at the top right of the screen.

    - Choose a name for your website (this will be part of the URL).

    - Set privacy (you can choose if you want everyone to see your site or only specific people).

    - Click on "Publish".

2. **Wix :**

    - Click the "Publish" button in the upper right corner.

    - Wix will give you a custom URL for your website.

    - You can also connect a custom domain if you have one.

    - Click on "Publish".

3. **Weebly for Education** :

- Click the "Publish" button at the top right.

- Choose a free Weebly subdomain or connect your own domain.

- Configure privacy and visibility.

- Click on "Publish".

Share your Website

Once your website is published, you'll want to share it with as many people as possible. Here are some ideas on how to do it.

1. **Email** :

- Send an email to your friends and family with the link to your website.

- Write a short message explaining what your page is about and why they should visit it.

Example :

```
Hola [Nombre],

Quiero compartir contigo mi
nueva página web sobre
dinosaurios. ¡He trabajado
mucho en ella y me encantaría
que la visitaras!

Aquí está el enlace:
[tu_pagina_web.com]

¡Espero que te guste!

Saludos,
[Tu Nombre]
```

2. **Social Networks** :

   - Post the link on your social media profiles (Facebook, Twitter, Instagram).

   - Use a short description and an attractive image to attract the attention of your followers.

Example :

```
Text                                    📋 Copiar código

¡Hola a todos! 🎉 Acabo de
lanzar mi nueva página web
sobre dinosaurios. 🦖🐾
Visítala aquí:
[tu_pagina_web.com] y descubre
datos fascinantes sobre estas
increíbles criaturas.
¡Déjame tus comentarios y dime
qué te parece!
```

3. **Class Presentations** :

   - If you are in school, you can ask your teacher if you can present your website to your classmates.

   - Show your page and explain how you created it and what content you have included.

4. **Posters and Flyers** :

    - Create posters or flyers with the link to your website and post them in visible places, such as your school's bulletin board.

    - Use bright colors and an eye-catching design to capture attention.

5. **Email Signature** :

    - Add the link to your website in your email signature.

    - Every time you send an email, people will see the link and can visit it.

Example :

```
Text                          📋 Copiar código

Saludos,
[Tu Nombre]
Visita mi página web:
[tu_pagina_web.com]
```

1. **Publish your Website** : Follow the instructions of your platform to publish your site.

2. **Send an Email** : Share the link of your page with at least five friends or family.

3. **Publish on Social Networks** : Share your page on your social network profiles.

4. **Create a Poster or Flyer** : Design a poster or flyer with the link to your page and place it in a visible place.

Congratulations! Now your website is published and shared with the world. In the next chapter, we will learn how to maintain and update your website so that it is always fresh and up-to-date. Keep it up!

Chapter 8: Maintain and Update

Creating a website is just the first step. To keep your site interesting and relevant, it is important to maintain and update it regularly. In this chapter, we will learn how to do it.

Why It is Important to Maintain and Update Your Website

1. **Keep your visitors interested** : By adding new and exciting content, your visitors will have a reason to return to your site.

2. **Fix Bugs** : Sometimes bugs can be overlooked at first. It is important to review and correct them.

3. **Update information** : Make sure the information on your site is always current and accurate.

Create an Update Calendar

Planning ahead will help you keep your website constantly updated.

1. **Weekly or Monthly Calendar** :

   - Decide how often you want to update your site (weekly, biweekly, monthly).

   - Mark days on your calendar to remind you when to make updates.

2. **New Content Ideas** :

   - **New Articles** : Write about new and exciting topics related to your site.

   - **Photos and Videos** : Add new photos and videos to keep your gallery updated.

   - **Events and News** : Post about recent events or news related to your topic.

Review and Improve Existing Content

Reviewing the content you already have is an important part of maintaining your website.

1. **Check your Spelling and Grammar** :

   - Make sure all content is written correctly.

   - Use tools like Grammarly or the spell checker on your platform.

2. **Update Outdated Information** :

   - Review your articles and pages to make sure all information is accurate and current.

   - Update any data or links that are no longer valid.

3. **Improve Content Quality** :

   - Add more details to existing articles.

   - Insert new images or graphics to make the content more attractive.

Add New Features

Adding new functionality can improve the visitor experience and make your site more interactive.

1. **Discussion Forums** :

   - Consider adding a forum where visitors can discuss topics related to your page.

2. **Newsletters** :

- Create a newsletter that visitors can subscribe to to receive regular updates about your site.

3. **Visual Improvements** :

- Change the layout or theme of your page from time to time to give it a fresh look.

- Add new templates or widgets according to the needs of your site.

Monitor your Page Traffic

Knowing how many people visit your page and which parts of your site are the most popular can help you improve.

1. **Analysis Tools** :

- Use tools like Google Analytics to monitor your page traffic.

- Check statistics to see which pages are the most visited and how much time visitors spend on your site.

2. **Comments and Feedback** :

- Read the comments left by your visitors and use their feedback to improve.

- Consider creating surveys to learn more about what they like and don't like.

1. **Create an Update Calendar** : Plan when and how you will update your site.

2. **Review and Improve Content** : Spend time reviewing and improving existing content.

3. **Add New Feature** : Consider adding a new feature to your site, such as a forum or newsletter.

4. **Monitor Traffic** : Use analytics tools to monitor your page traffic and adjust your content based on the results.

Amazing work! Now you know how to maintain and update your website so that it is always interesting and attractive. In the next chapter, we'll give you some advanced tips to take your website to the next level. Let's go for more!

Chapter 9: Additional Resources

To help you continue to improve and expand your website, here is a list of additional resources you can use. These resources will provide you with tools, inspiration, and support on your journey as a website builder.

Design and Creativity Resources

1. **Graphic Design Tools** :

   - **Canva** : [Canva](https://www.canva.com) is an easy-to-use online tool that allows you to create graphics and designs impressive for your website.

   - **Pixlr** : [Pixlr](https://pixlr.com) is a free online photo editor that offers many Photoshop-like features.

2. **Image and Video Bank** :

   - **Pixabay** : [Pixabay](https://pixabay.com) offers a wide collection of free images and videos that you can use on your page.

   - **Unsplash** : [Unsplash](https://unsplash.com) provides high-quality royalty-free photos.

3. **Fonts and Typography** :

   - **Google Fonts** : [Google Fonts](https://fonts.google.com) offers a wide variety of free fonts that you can integrate on your site to improve typography.

   - **FontSpace** : [FontSpace](https://www.fontspace.com) is a library of free fonts where you can find unique styles.

Learning Resources

1. **Tutorials and Online Courses** :

   - **W3Schools** : [W3Schools](https://www.w3schools.com) offers free tutorials on HTML, CSS, JavaScript, and more.

- **Khan Academy** : [Khan Academy](https://www.khanacademy.org) has free courses on programming and design Web.

2. **Books and Guides** :

- **"HTML & CSS: Design and Build Websites "by Jon Duckett** : A colorful, easy-to-understand book that explains the basics of HTML and CSS.

- **"JavaScript for Kids : A Playful Introduction to Programming " by Nick Morgan** : A fun and accessible to learn JavaScript.

Development tools

1. **Code Editors** :

- **Visual Studio Code** : [Visual Studio Code](https://code.visualstudio.com) is a free and very popular among developers.

- **Sublime Text** : [Sublime Text](https://www.sublimetext.com) is a lightweight and powerful code editor.

2. **Debugging and Testing** :

- **Browser Developer Tools** : Browsers like Chrome and Firefox have built-in development tools that allow you to debug and test your code.

- **JSFiddle** : [JSFiddle](https://jsfiddle.net) is an online tool that allows you to test and share HTML, CSS code snippets and JavaScript.

Communities and Forums

1. **Stack Overflow** : [Stack Overflow](https://stackoverflow.com) is a community where you can ask questions and get answers from other developers.

- **Web Development Forums** : Look for specific forums on web development where you can share your experiences and learn from others.

2. **Groups on Social Networks** :

- **Facebook Groups** : Join web development groups on Facebook to connect with other creators and share ideas.

- **Reddit** : Subreddits like [r/ webdev](https://www.reddit.com/r/webdev) are great for discussing web development topics and getting help.

Inspirational Resources

1. **Design Galleries** :

   - **Awwwards** : [Awwwards](https://www.awwwards.com) is a gallery featuring the best website designs in the world.

   - **Dribbble** : [Dribbble](https://dribbble.com) is a community of designers where you can see inspiring work and get ideas for your site.

2. **Blogs and Websites** :

   - **Smashing Magazine** : [Smashing Magazine](https://www.smashingmagazine.com) offers articles and resources on web design and development.

   - **CSS- Tricks** : [CSS- Tricks](https://css-tricks.com) is a blog full of tutorials and tricks to improve your CSS skills.

1. **Explore Design Tools** : Try out some of the graphic design tools and find the ones you like best.

2. **Access Tutorials** : Choose an online tutorial or course and learn something new about web development.

3. **Join a Community** : Find an online community that interests you and join to start sharing your experiences and learning from others.

Fantastic! You now have a toolbox full of additional resources to help you improve and expand your website. Keep exploring and learning, and you'll see your website grow and improve over time. Good luck on your digital adventure!

Conclusion

Congratulations on reaching the end of this book! Now you have all the tools and knowledge necessary to create, maintain and improve your own website. Throughout these chapters, you have learned from the basics to advanced techniques that will help you stand out in the digital world.

Summary of what was learned

1. **Introduction to Web Pages** :

    - You understood what a web page is and why it is important.

    - You learned about the different types of web pages and how they work.

2. **Planning your Website** :

    - You discovered how to plan your website according to your interests and needs.

    - You created a sketch and organized the sections and content of your site.

3. **Tools and Programs** :

    - You explored various platforms and tools that you can use to design and build your website.

    - You got familiar with Google Sites , Wix , Weebly , and more.

4. **Design of your Website** :

    - You learned how to create an attractive and functional design.

    - You used templates and customized the design to reflect your style and goals.

5. **Add Content** :

    - You added text, images, videos and other multimedia elements to your page.

- You learned to organize and present content in a clear and attractive way.

6. **Make your Page Interactive :**

    - Added interactive elements such as links, forms, comments and widgets.

    - You improved the user experience and encouraged the participation of your visitors.

7. **Publish and Share :**

    - You published your website and shared it with your audience.

    - You used strategies to promote your site and attract visitors.

8. **Maintain and Update :**

    - You discovered the importance of keeping your website updated.

    - Created an update schedule and reviewed and improved your existing content.

9. **Additional Resources :**

    - You accessed a variety of additional resources to continue learning and improving.

    - You found inspiration and useful tools for your continued development.

Next steps

- **Keep Learning** : The world of web development is constantly evolving. Keep learning new techniques and tools to stay up to date.

- **Experiment and Create** : Don't be afraid to experiment with new ideas and designs. Practice and creativity will help you continually improve.

- **Share your Knowledge** : Help others learn by sharing your knowledge and experiences. You can teach your friends, family or even create your own blog or tutorial channel.

A Final Message

Creating a website is like building a bridge to the digital world. Through your website, you can share your interests, ideas and projects with people around the world. Remember that every step you take on this journey brings you closer to becoming an expert in web development.

Thank you for joining us on this journey! We are excited to see the amazing web pages you will create. Good luck and continue exploring the fascinating world of the web!

And so we conclude our book! Now, armed with all this knowledge, it's your turn to shine in the digital world! Go, young web developer!

Important notes

Before we finish, here are some important notes to keep in mind while working on your website:

1. **Online Security** :

    - Never share personal information such as your address, phone number or passwords on your website.

    - If you allow comments or interactions, monitor the content to ensure it is appropriate.

2. **Copyright and Fair Use** :

    - Make sure all content (images, videos, music) you use on your page has the appropriate licenses.

    - Use free and royalty-free resources when possible, and give credit to the original authors if necessary.

3. **Accessibility** :

    - Design your page so that it is accessible to everyone, including people with disabilities.

    - Use alt text for images and make sure your site is keyboard navigable.

4. **Privacy** :

    - If you collect information from your visitors (such as through contact forms), be sure to respect their privacy.

    - Do not share your visitors' information with third parties without their consent.

5. **Mobile Optimization** :

    - Make sure your website looks good and works correctly on mobile devices.

    - Use responsive designs that adapt to different screen sizes.

6. **Testing and Feedback** :

   - Test your website on different browsers and devices to make sure it works correctly.

   - Ask friends and family to review your site and provide feedback.

7. **Regular Update** :

   - Keep your content updated so your page remains relevant and attractive.

   - Review and improve your site periodically to fix errors and add new features.

8. **Usability and Navigation** :

   - Design your page to be easy to navigate.

   - Use clear menus and links that take your visitors to the information they are looking for.

9. **Performance and Speed** :

   - Optimize images and other files so your page loads quickly.

   - Avoid excessive use of animations or elements that can slow down your site.

10. **Fun and Creativity** :

   - Have fun creating your website! Let your creativity shine and experiment with different ideas and designs.

Remember, your website is an extension of you and your interests. Take care of it and keep learning to make it better and better. Good luck and enjoy the process!